THE EARTH
IS PAINTED
GREEN

THE EARTH IS PAINTED GREEN

A GARDEN OF POEMS ABOUT OUR PLANET

Edited by Barbara Brenner

Illustrated by S.D. Schindler

A BYRON PREISS BOOK

SCHOLASTIC INC.
NEW YORK

Compilation copyright © 1994
by Byron Preiss Visual Publications, Inc.

Illustrations copyright © 1994
by S.D. Schindler and Byron Preiss Visual Publications, Inc.

"The Deep Green Forest," copyright © 1994 by Tanya Dreskin.
"The Moss," copyright © 1994 by Leila Dreskin.

*Special thanks to Jean Feiwel, Phoebe Yeh, Claire Counihan,
Michelle Cimini, and Paige Gillies.*

EDITOR: *Gillian Bucky*
ASSOCIATE EDITOR: *Kathy Huck*
BOOK DESIGN: *Pearl Lau*
COVER DESIGN: *Dean Motter*

Library of Congress Cataloging-in-Publication Data
The Earth is painted green; a garden of poems about our planet /
edited by Barbara Brenner; illustrated by S.D. Schindler.
p. cm.
"A Byron Preiss book."
Summary: An illustrated collection of poems from around the world
about various aspects of green life on earth.
ISBN 0-590-45134-0
I. Earth—Juvenile poetry. [1. Earth—Poetry. 2. Nature—Poetry.
3. Poetry—Collections.]
I. Brenner, Barbara, II. Schindler, S.D., ill.
PN6109.97E27 1994   93-21466
808.81'936—dc20   CIP
                                      AC

12 11 10 9 8 7 6 5 4 3 2 1   4 5 6 7 8 9/9

Printed in the U.S.A.   37

First Scholastic printing, March 1994

The illustrations in this book are watercolor paintings.

To Claudia Lewis
—B.B.

CONTENTS

EARTH GREEN

I'm Glad . . .
Anonymous
2

I Don't Know Why
Myra Cohn Livingston
6

Earth Song
David McCord
3

The Deep Green Forest
Tanya Dreskin
7

Green Stems
Margaret Wise Brown
4

Green Song
Lillian Morrison
8

Oak Leaf Plate
Mary Ann Hoberman
5

To Look at Any Thing
John Moffitt
9

FIRST GREEN

First One Out of Bed
X. J. Kennedy
10

Directions
Onitsura
13

Fueled
Marcie Hans
11

Silver Lining
Sanpū
13

Spring Talk
David McCord
12

Snowman
Shel Silverstein
14

White Floating Clouds
Sia
15

Tree Green

Blow-up
X. J. Kennedy
16

Sumac Whistle
Robert Newton Peck
19

Two Ancient Pine-Trees
Ryoto
17

Five Chants
David McCord
20 – 21

Strange Tree
Elizabeth Madox Roberts
17

Poplars
Edward Bliss Reed
22

Be Different to Trees
Mary Carolyn Davies
18

Evergreen
Eve Merriam
23

The Moss
Leila Dreskin
18

The Comb of Trees
Claudia Lewis
24

The Tempter
Translated by Harold Henderson
19

Counting-out Rhyme
Edna St. Vincent Millay
25

Tree-Sleeping
Robert P. Tristram Coffin
26

PLANTING GREEN

The Grass on the Mountain
Transcribed by Mary Austin
28

Azalea
Charlotte Zolotow
29

Grass
Kathleen Fraser
29

Green With Envy
Eve Merriam
30

On the Problem of Growing
a Head of Lettuce
in a Very Small Garden
Louis Phillips
30

Mushrooms
Robert Newton Peck
31

weeds
Valerie Worth
32

dandelion
Valerie Worth
32

Accidentally
Maxine W. Kumin
33

GROWING GREEN

The Song of a Dream
Aztec Indians
34

Is It Raining Up There
Papago
34

The Corn Grows Up
Navajo Indians
35

Nicely, Nicely
Zuni Corn Ceremony
35

Yellow Weed
Lilian Moore
36

Tiger Lily
David McCord
37

Poppies
Roy Scheele
37

Tulip
Robert Wallace
38

Flowers at Night
Aileen Fisher
38

Blue Magic
Eleanor Farjeon
39

Violets
Charlotte Zolotow
39

Kudzu
Eve Merriam
40

SUMMER GREEN

The Garden Hose
Beatrice Janosco
41

The Waking
Theodore Roethke
42

Strange Houses
Carl Withers
43

Watermelon
Ted Joans
43

A Gopher in the Garden
Jack Prelutsky
44

Song Against Broccoli
Roy Blount, Jr.
44

Potato
Vasko Popa
45

Nocturn Cabbage
Carl Sandburg
45

The Man in the Onion Bed
John Ciardi
46

Mushrooms Are Umbrellas
Arnold Spilka
46

Millions of Strawberries
Genevieve Taggard
47

Mr. Bidery's Spidery Garden
David McCord
48 – 49

lawnmower
Valerie Worth
50

Poison Ivy
Louis Phillips
50

HARVEST GREEN

Now in Late Autumn
Taigi
51

pumpkin
Valerie Worth
52

acorn
Valerie Worth
53

Oh! I Ate Them All
Shiki
53

Apple
Nan Fry
53

Ladybug, Be Good
Norma Farber
54

Harvest
Carl Sandburg
55

Autumn Leaves
Aileen Fisher
56

The Leaves Fall Down
Margaret Wise Brown
56

Leaves
Soseki
56

The Harvest Moon
Ted Hughes
57

LAST GREEN

Yase: September
Gary Snyder
58

Maple Sweet
Carl Carmer
61

The Mist and All
Dixie Willson
59

The Tree on the Corner
Lilian Moore
62

First White Snow of Fall
Basho
59

Buds
Elizabeth Coatsworth
62

Forever Green

Earth
John Hall Wheelock
63

To Nature Seekers
Robert W. Chambers
64

Hurt No Living Thing
Christina Rossetti
64

Progress
Connie Martin
65

And They Lived Happily
Ever After for a While
John Ciardi
66–67

The Flower-Fed Buffaloes
Vachel Lindsay
68

The Great Auk's Ghost
Ralph Hodgson
69

A Prayer for a Carpenter
Louis Phillips
69

Choose a Color
Jacqueline Sweeney
70–71

This Pretty Planet (A Round)
John Forster and Tom Chapin
72

Valentine for Earth
Frances Frost
73

Index of Authors
74–75

Index of Titles
76–77

Index of First Lines
78–79

Acknowledgments
80–81

EARTH GREEN

People write poems to express big ideas in a few
carefully chosen words. We know that green
plants may be the most important living things
on our planet; and without plants to trap the
sun's energy, there would be no life on Earth as
we know it. The poems in "Earth Green" consider
the magic and power of Earth's green things.

I'm Glad . . .

I'm glad the sky is painted blue,
    And the earth is painted green,
With such a lot of nice fresh air
    All sandwiched in between.

Anonymous

Earth Song

Let me dry you, says the desert;
Let me wet you, says the sea.
If that's the way they talk, why don't
They talk that way to me?

Let me fan you, says the wind;
Oh, let me cool you, says the rain.
Let me bury you, the snow says;
Let me dye you with the stain

Of sunset, says the evening;
Let me float you, says the lake;
Let me drift you, says the river.
Says the temblor, let me shake

You. *Freeze* you, says the glacier;
Let me burn you, says the sun.
I don't know what the moon says,
Or that star—the green pale one.

David McCord

Green Stems

Little things that crawl and creep
In the green grass forests,
Deep in their long-stemmed world
Where ferns uncurl
To a greener world
Beneath the leaves above them;
And every flower upon its stem
Blows above them there
The bottom of a geranium,
The back side of a trillium,
The belly of a bumblebee
Is all they see, these little things
Down so low
Where no bird sings
Where no winds blow,
Deep in their long-stemmed world.

Margaret Wise Brown

Oak Leaf Plate

Oak leaf plate
Acorn cup
Raindrop tea
Drink it up!

Sand for salt
Mud for pie
Twiggy chops
Fine to fry.

Sticks for bread
Stones for meat
Grass for greens
Time to eat!

Mary Ann Hoberman

I Don't Know Why

I don't know why
    the sky is blue
    or why the raindrops
    splatter through

    or why the grass
    is wet with dew . . . do you?

I don't know why
    the sun is round
    or why a seed grows
    in the ground

    or why the thunder
    makes a sound . . . do you?

I don't know why
    the clouds are white
    or why the moon
    shines very bright

    or why the air
    turns black at night . . . do you?

Myra Cohn Livingston

The Deep Green Forest

The deep green forest is dark and quiet;
Ferns grow all along the trail.
Silence.

Tanya Dreskin, age 7

Green Song

I can never get my fill
of chlorophyll,
of glory-filled weather
when the air is clear and dry,
when grasshoppers in their gauntlets
hop along high
and bright-winged butterflies
delight the eye,
when sun and breeze combine
to make the landscape shine
and green's the major color
against an azure sky.

Lillian Morrison

To Look at Any Thing

To look at any thing,
If you would know that thing,
You must look at it long:
To look at this green and say
'I have seen spring in these
Woods,' will not do—you must
Be the thing you see:
You must be the dark snakes of
Stems and ferny plumes of leaves,
You must enter in
To the small silences between
The leaves,
You must take your time
And touch the very peace
They issue from.

John Moffitt

FIRST GREEN

From ancient times, people all over the world
have held celebrations to welcome the moment
when plants begin to show new growth.
In this section, poets celebrate the first green.

First One Out of Bed

Up through the ground,
  Having just awoke,
With a leap and a bound
  Early Crocus broke,

Took a quick look around,
  Shouted: *Holy smoke!*
All the world's sleeping sound!
  Up jumped Artichoke.

X. J. Kennedy

Fueled

Fueled
by a million
man-made
wings of fire—
the rocket tore a tunnel
through the sky—
and everybody cheered.

Fueled
only by a thought from God—
the seedling
urged its way
through the thicknesses of black—
and as it pierced
the heavy ceiling of the soil—
and launched itself
up into outer space—
no
one
even
clapped.

Marcie Hans

Spring Talk

Jack-in-the-pulpit: Where are you, Jack?
"He's out for a minute; he'll be right back."
Did you hear that? Real pulpit talk:
You hear it only the first spring walk.

Hello, skunk cabbage! Where's old skunk?
"He's rolled up here in the upper bunk."
Of course he isn't—he can't be. Who
Ever heard of cabbage with bunks for two?

Well, dogtooth violet, and how's that tooth?
"It aches a bit, to tell the truth."
Now you heard *that*: he says it aches.
Let's ask wake-robin when robin wakes,

And toadstools where the toads have gone.
"They all went home. They leave at dawn.
Wake robin, though, and hear him sing."
Who wants to walk with me next spring?

David McCord

Directions

Eyes, side to side;
nose, up-and-down.
Spring flowers!

Onitsura

Silver Lining

May rains pour:
and now the frogs are swimming
at my door!

Sanpū

13

Snowman

'Twas the first day of the springtime
And the snowman stood alone
As the winter snows were melting,
And the pine trees seemed to groan
"Ah, you poor sad smiling snowman
You'll be melting by and by."
Said the snowman, "What a pity,
For I'd like to see July.
Yes, I'd like to see July, and please don't ask me why,
But I'd like to, yes I'd like to, oh I'd like to see July."

Chirped a robin, just arriving,
"Seasons come and seasons go,
And the greatest ice must crumble
When it's flowers' time to grow.
And as one thing is beginning
So another thing must die,
And there's never been a snowman
Who has ever seen July.
No, they never see July, no matter how they try.
No, they never ever, never ever, never see July."

But the snowman sniffed his carrot nose
And said, "At least I'll try,"
And he bravely smiled his frosty smile
And blinked his coal-black eye.
And there he stood and faced the sun
A blazin' from the sky—
And I really cannot tell you
If he ever saw July.
Did he ever see July? You can guess as well as I,
If he ever, if he never, if he ever saw July.

Shel Silverstein

White Floating Clouds

White floating clouds,
Clouds like the plains,
Come and water the earth.
Sun embrace the earth
that she may be fruitful.
Moon, lion of the north,
Bear of the west,
Badger of the south,
Wolf of the east,
Eagle of the heavens,
Shrew of the earth,
Elder war hero,
Warriors of the six mountains of the world,
Intercede with the cloud people for us
That they may water the earth.

Sia

TREE GREEN

Trees are among Earth's oldest life-forms—even
older than the dinosaurs! There are thousands
of different species of trees. No two are
exactly alike, just as no two poems about
trees are exactly the same.

Blow-up

Our cherry tree
Unfolds whole loads
Of pink-white bloom—
It just explodes.

For three short days
Its petals last.
Oh, what a waste.
But what a blast.

X. J. Kennedy

Two Ancient Pine-Trees

Two ancient pine-trees . . .
   A pair of gnarled
   And sturdy hands
With ten green fingers

Ryoto

Strange Tree

Away beyond the Jarboe house
I saw a different kind of tree.
Its trunk was old and large and bent,
And I could feel it look at me.

The road was going on and on
Beyond to reach some other place.
I saw a tree that looked at me,
And yet it did not have a face.

It looked at me with all its limbs;
It looked at me with all its bark.
The yellow wrinkles on its sides
Were bent and dark.

And then I ran to get away,
But when I stopped to turn and see,

The tree was bending to the side
And leaning out to look at me.

Elizabeth Madox Roberts

17

Be Different to Trees

The talking oak
To the ancients spoke.

But any tree
Will talk to me.

What truths I know
I garnered so.

But those who want to talk and tell,
  And those who will not listeners be,
Will never hear a syllable
  From out the lips of any tree.

Mary Carolyn Davies

The Moss

Once there was a tree
And the moss grew on it
And moss growing on it
Was so even.
It was like grass someone cut
with a lawnmower.
The trunk of the tree
was almost as hard as a rock.
And the moss was as soft as thistledown.

Leila Dreskin, age 5

18

The Tempter

Plum blossoms swaying:
"Here! Here! Steal this one!"— is that
what the moon's saying?

Translated by Harold Henderson

Sumac Whistle

April's here, to cut for me
A whistle. Find a sumac tree
Out beyond the creek that's lean,
I'd say finger-thick, and green.

Search a section near a crotch
To punch a blowhole. Cut a notch
Like so. Then it should be a cinch
To slip the bark sleeve half an inch.

Bucket soak it overnight
So the bond gets locked on tight
Enough to hold. It's smooth and round
To blow a sumac whistle sound.

Draw a breath that's full and deep
Or you won't produce a peep
Of a yellow chick. That's right,
Put it to your mouth real tight.

And blow! With all your might and main.
You'll stab some poor soul's ear a pain.
And jump? He'll leave his shoes beneath
His feet. Or maybe pop his teeth.

You won't make friends but enemies
For yourself and sumac trees.
But there's no sweeter April toy—
A sumac whistle for a boy.

Robert Newton Peck

Five Chants

Every time I climb a tree
Every time I climb a tree
Every time I climb a tree
I scrape a leg
Or skin a knee
And every time I climb a tree
I find some ants
Or dodge a bee
And get the ants
All over me

And every time I climb a tree
Where have you been?
They say to me
But don't they know that I am free
Every time I climb a tree?
I like it best
To spot a nest
That has an egg
or maybe three

And then I skin
The other leg
But every time I climb a tree
I see a lot of things to see
Swallows rooftops and TV
And all the fields and farms there be
Every time I climb a tree
Though climbing may be good for ants
It isn't awfully good for pants
But still it's pretty good for me
Every time I climb a tree

David McCord

21

Poplars

The poplar is a lonely tree,
It has no branches spreading wide
Where birds may sing or squirrels hide.
It throws no shadow on the grass
Tempting the wayfarers who pass
To stop and sit there quietly.

The poplar is a slender tree,
It has no boughs where children try
To climb far off into the sky.

To hold a swing, it's far too weak,
Too small it is for hide-and-seek,
Friendless, forsaken it must be.

The poplar is a restless tree,
At every breeze its branches bend
And signal to the child, "Come, friend."
Its leaves forever whispering
To thrush and robin, "Stay and sing,"
They pass. It quivers plaintively.

Poplars are lonely. They must grow
Close to each other in a row.

Edward Bliss Reed

Evergreen

Hemlock and pine
stand in July
grassy steeples
against the sky.

Sequoia and yew
October days short
green shadows lengthen
over the court.

Spruce and cypress
December winds blow
emerald palaces
shining in snow.

Cedar and fir
March freshets and rains
whatever the season
green remains.

Juniper conifer constancy
evergreen evergreen evergreen grow
evergreen evergreen ever green grow.

Eve Merriam

23

The Comb of Trees
A Secret Sign Along the Way

Riding to Rock Creek
for our picnics
we swing around
a certain curve
and then I see it—

Standing high
on a mountain ridge
a little row
of firs, with trunks
tall and bare,
lined up one by one—
a comb
against the sky.

As we draw near
each time
I wonder—

it . . . ?
Is it . . . ?

Then we turn—

Yes! It's there!

No storm
has wrecked my comb,
no lumberjack
has chopped it down—

All's well
still
(a while?)
up there.

Claudia Lewis

24

Counting-out Rhyme

Silver bark of beech, and sallow
Bark of yellow birch and yellow
     Twig of willow.

Stripe of green in moosewood maple,
Colour seen in leaf of apple,
     Bark of popple.

Wood of popple pale as moonbeam,
Wood of oak for yoke and barn-beam,
     Wood of hornbeam.

Silver bark of beech, and hollow
Stem of elder, tall and yellow
     Twig of willow.

Edna St. Vincent Millay

Tree-Sleeping

When I was small and trees were high,
I loved to sleep out nights by the sea,
A spruce that held up half the sky
Had boughs like beds where I could lie,
So thick the twigs I could not slide
Through to earth, and at my side
The evening star lay close to me.

The night came over the ocean slow,
A wind came up from nowhere there,
I felt my tree go to and fro
Until my bed was wholly air,
I lay on music grave and deep,
Moved on oceans of holy sleep,
With great stars tangled in my hair.

A sea-bird on a snowy wing
Came down with treble cries,
Alighted on my bed, this thing
Woke me with wide surprise,
Flew off with golden talons curled,
And there on the blue edge of the world
The young sun looked me in the eyes.

Robert P. Tristram Coffin

PLANTING GREEN

People have different ways of planting seeds—just
before a rain; by the light of the moon;
with a chant. The poetry of many cultures
celebrates planting time and the wish
for a good crop.

The Grass on the Mountain

From the Paiute American Indian

Oh, long long
The snow has possessed the mountains.

The deer have come down and the big-horn,
They have followed the Sun to the south
To feed on the mesquite pods and the bunch grass.
Loud are the thunderdrums
In the tents of the mountains.
Oh, long long
Have we eaten chia seeds
And dried deer's flesh of the summer killing.
We are wearied of our huts
And the smoky smell of our garments.

We are sick with the desire of the sun
And the grass on the mountain.

Transcribed by Mary Austin

Azalea

I feel as though
this bush were grown
especially for me.
I feel as though
I almost am
this little flowering tree.

Charlotte Zolotow

Grass

Grass!
That's my grass,
green poking, cool in hot summer
and yellow under the washtub.
From there I've seen stars falling.
The grass is my second skin.
Drawers opening, spilling with green. Or doors.
Each blade the entrance to the grass city.
Lie in it. Open slowly to it. The creatures moving there
are among endless waving forests of green.
The names of grasses have their own smell:
beach grass, beard grass, Bengal grass, bent, bent grass,
running barefoot grass
Bermuda, blue joint, and bog grass
Bristly foxtail
Bunch grass in bunches
Canary grass singing
China grass, ping! (and tiny figures floating in it)

Kathleen Fraser

29

Green With Envy

"I,"
stalks the pale asparagus,
"have green fingernails."

"My hair,"
tops the carrot,
"is green."

"Only I,"
lettuce leaves for the last,
"have a heart of green."

Eve Merriam

On the Problem of Growing a Head of Lettuce in a Very Small Garden

Rapid
Rabid
Rabbits
Grab it.

Louis Phillips

Mushrooms

Little lowly people of the earth
Who live unseen beneath the buried brown,
Will show their heads, a small community;
And bicker in their crowded little town.

A colony, all leghorn white and smooth.
Make appearance on a single day;
And raise their children all about as chicks.
Up they grow, and then to move away.

One mushroom boy has freckles on his face.
His gangled legs will wobble in the dew
As if to say he does not care to dance
At all, despite his party suit is new.

Across the leafy ballroom, nests of girls
Await, all gowned in crimson, yellow, green
Heads together, whispering of him;
Each one hoping that she will be seen.

The party is disrupted when a squirrel
Appears, to nibble at a mushroom treat.
His tiny paws reach out to break a piece
From off the edge, to turn it; then to eat.

The squirrel sees me, but does not scamper off.
Perhaps he knows he need not be too shy.
We mushroom fanciers are gentle folk.
We come to visit mushrooms, squirrel and I.

Robert Newton Peck

weeds

In the rough places,
Along concrete curbs,
Up railroad banks,
Next to brick buildings,
Weeds will grow;
And no one cares
If they live there,
Year after year:
Quietly attending
To roots, stalks,
Or even, above
Dusty leaves, a few
Dim stars of flowers.

Valerie Worth

dandelion

Out of
Green space,
A sun:
Bright for
A day, burning
Away to
A husk, a
Cratered moon:

Burst
In a week
To dust:
Seeding
The infinite
Lawn with
Its starry
Smithereens.

Valerie Worth

Accidentally

Once—I didn't mean to,
but that
was that—
I yawned in the sunshine
and swallowed a gnat.

I'd rather eat mushrooms
and bullfrogs' legs,
I'd rather have pepper
all over my eggs

than open my mouth
on a sleepy day
and close on a gnat
going down that way.

It tasted sort of salty.
It didn't hurt a bit.
I accidentally ate a gnat.
and that
was
it!

Maxine W. Kumin

GROWING GREEN

If you sow seeds, plant trees, raise flowers,
or grow vegetables, you harvest much more than
what you plant. These poems capture the experience
of growing things—the fun . . . *and* the frustrations!

The Song of a Dream

Now, my friends, please hear:
it is the song of a dream:
each spring the gold young corn
gives us life;
the ripened corn gives us refreshment;
to know that the hearts of our friends
are true is to put around us
a necklace of precious stones.

Aztec Indians

Is It Raining Up There

It is raining up there
Under the mountain,
The corn tassels are shaking
Under the mountain,
The horns of the child corn are glistening.

Papago

The Corn Grows Up

The corn grows up.
The waters of the dark clouds drop, drop.
The rain descends.
The waters from the corn leaves drop, drop.
The rain descends.
The waters from the plants drop, drop.
The corn grows up.
The waters of the dark mists drop, drop.

Navajo Indians

Nicely, Nicely

Nicely, nicely, nicely, away in the east,
the rain clouds care for the little corn
    plants
as a mother cares for her baby.

Zuni Corn Ceremony

Yellow Weed

How did you get here,
weed?
Who brought your seed?

Did it lift
on the wind and
sail
and drift
from a far and yellow
field?

Was your seed a
burr,
a sticky burr that
clung to a
fox's
furry tail?

Did it fly with a
bird
who liked to feed
on the tasty
seed
of the yellow
weed?

How did you come?

Lilian Moore

Tiger Lily

The tiger lily is a panther,
Orange to black spot:
Her tongue is the velvet pretty anther,
And she's in the vacant lot.

The cool day lilies grow beside her,
But they are done now and dead,
And between them a little spider
Hangs from a thread.

David McCord

Poppies

The light in them stands as clear as water
drawn from a well.
When the breeze moves across them they totter.
You half expect them to spill.

Roy Scheele

Tulip

It digs the air with green blades,
scooping, curled,
then thrusts out colored gear
in the upper-world

to tap sun and bees and suck
such fuels down
as run its dark machinery
without sound.

Robert Wallace

Flowers at Night

Some flowers close their petals,
blue and red and bright,
and go to sleep all tucked away
inside themselves at night.

Some flowers leave their petals
like windows open wide
so they can watch the goings-on
of stars and things outside.

Aileen Fisher

Blue Magic

In the woods the bluebells seem
Like a blue and magic dream,
Blue water, light and air
 Flow among them there.

But the eager girl who pulls
Bluebells up in basketfuls
When she gets them home will find
 The magic left behind.

Eleanor Farjeon

Violets

Someone is coming
down the road
and they may buy
a bunch of our violets
purple and sweet
smelling of spring.
But we won't tell
the secret place
where they grow.
No one will know
the tall grass
where we found them.
No one can buy
the feeling of the hot sun
on our hair
as we picked them.
It is only the flowers themselves
the violets
purple and sweet
they'll take away.

Charlotte Zolotow

Kudzu

When kudzu seed the sower sows,
how it grows and overgrows.

Starting in one garden plot,
soon it's in the next-door lot,

twining round the neighbors' door,
creeping to their second floor,

at their chimney, climbing higher
to TV's antenna wire,

past the church's topmost spire,
kudzu to the sky and skyer.

Eve Merriam

SUMMER GREEN

The secret of finding "green" at summertime
is in looking closely at the colors of summer's green.
In these poems, writers peek inside blooming
plants and flowers and share their experience
in word pictures—poems.

The Garden Hose

In the gray evening
I see a long green serpent
With its tail in the dahlias.

It lies in loops across the grass
And drinks softly at the faucet.

I can hear it swallow.

Beatrice Janosco

The Waking

I strolled across
An open field;
The sun was out;
Heat was happy.

This way! This way!
The wren's throat shimmered,
Either to other,
The blossoms sang.

The stones sang,
The little ones did,
And flowers jumped
Like small goats.

A ragged fringe
Of daisies waved;
I wasn't alone
In a grove of apples.

Far in the wood
A nestling sighed;
The dew loosened
Its morning smells.

I came where the river
Ran over stones:
My ears knew
An early joy.

And all the waters
Of all the streams
Sang in my veins
That summer day.

Theodore Roethke

Strange Houses

There was a little green house:
And inside the little green house
There was a little brown house;
And inside the little brown house
There was a little yellow house;
And inside the little yellow house
There was a little white house;
And inside the little white house
There was a little sweet heart.
                              —A walnut.

Out in the field
There is a green house:
Inside that green house
There is a white house;
Inside that white house
There is a red house;
And inside that red house
There's a lot of little white babies.
                              —A watermelon.

Carl Withers

Watermelon

Its got a good shape/the outside color is green/its one
          of them foods from Africa
its got stripes sometimes like a zebra or Florida prison
          pants
Its bright red inside/ the black eyes are flat and shiney/
          it wont make you fat
Its got heavy liquid weight/the sweet taste is unique/some
          people are shamed of it/
I aint afraid to eat it/indoors or out/its soul food
          thing/Watermelon is what I'm
talking about Yeah watermelon is what I'm talking about
          Watermelon

Ted Joans

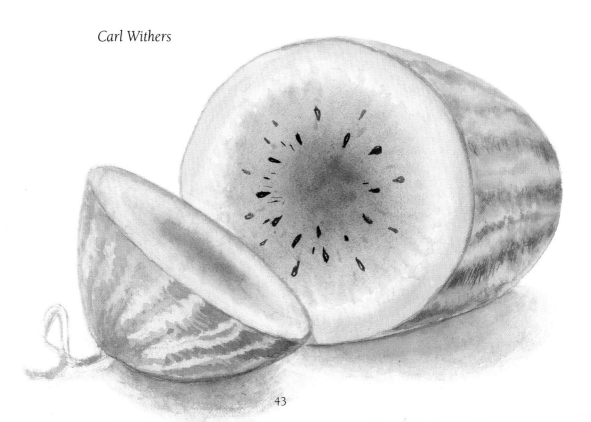

43

A Gopher in the Garden

There's a gopher in the garden, and he's eating all the onions,
and he's eating all the broccoli and all the beets and beans,
and he's eating all the carrots, all the corn and cauliflower,
all the parsley, peas and pumpkins, all the radishes and greens.

At breakfast, lunch or dinnertime the gopher is no loafer
and he quickly will devour everything before his eyes.
He does not even hesitate to eat a cabbage twice his weight,
or a watermelon five or six or seven times his size.

Jack Prelutsky

Song Against Broccoli

The local groceries are all out of broccoli.
Loccoli.

Roy Blount, Jr.

Nocturn Cabbage

Cabbages catch at the moon.
    It is late summer, no rain, the pack of the soil
    cracks open, it is a hard summer.

In the night the cabbages catch at the moon, the
    leaves drip silver, the rows of cabbages are
    series of little silver waterfalls in the moon.

Carl Sandburg

Potato

Mysterious murky
Face of Earth

He speaks
With midnight fingers
The language of eternal noon

He sprouts
With unexpected dawns
In his larder of memories

All because
In his heart
The sun sleeps

Vasko Popa
(Translated from the Serbo-
Croatian by Anne Pennington)

The Man in the Onion Bed

I met a man in an onion bed.
He was crying so hard his eyes were red.
And the tears ran off the end of his nose
As he ate his way down the onion rows.

He ate and he cried, but for all his tears
He sang: "Sweet onions, oh my dears!
I love you, I do, and you love me,
But you make me as sad as a man can be."

John Ciardi

Mushrooms Are Umbrellas

Mushrooms are umbrellas

for

ladybugs

and

their

fellas.

Arnold Spilka

Millions of Strawberries

Marcia and I went over the curve,
Eating our way down
Jewels of strawberries we didn't deserve,
Eating our way down.
Till our hands were sticky, and our lips painted,
And over us the hot day fainted,
And we saw snakes,
And got scratched,
And a lust overcame us for the red unmatched
Small buds of berries,
Till we lay down—
Eating our way down—
And rolled in the berries like two little dogs,
Rolled
In the late gold.
And gnats hummed,
And it was cold,
And home we went, home without a berry,
Painted red and brown,
Eating our way down.

Genevieve Taggard

Mr. Bidery's Spidery Garden

Poor old Mr. Bidery.
His garden's awfully spidery:
Bugs use it as a hidery.

In April it was seedery,
By May a mess of weedery;
And oh, the bugs! How greedery.

White flowers out or buddery,
Potatoes made it spuddery;
And when it rained, what muddery!

June days grow long and shaddery;
Bullfrog forgets his taddery;
The spider legs his laddery.

With cabbages so odory,
Snapdragon soon explodery,
At twilight all is toadary.

Young corn still far from foddery,
No sign of goldenrodery,
Yet feeling low and doddery

Is poor old Mr. Bidery,
His garden lush and spidery,
His apples green, not cidery.

Pea-picking *is* so poddery!

David McCord

lawnmower

The lawnmower
Grinds its teeth
Over the grass,
Spitting out a thick
Green spray;

Its head is too full
Of iron and oil
To know
What it throws
Away:

The lawn's whole
Crop of chopped,
Soft,
Delicious
Green hay.

Valerie Worth

Poison Ivy

Personally,
I think it's silly
To always gather
Daffodillies.

What's wrong with
Poison Ivy?
We've barely scratched
The surface there.

Though once you've gathered
Poison Ivy,
You'll be scratching everywhere.

Louis Phillips

HARVEST GREEN

Harvesting is a joyous time. There's the thrill of
harvesting the crop—picking and feasting
and, best of all, sharing nature's bounty
and poems about it.

Now in Late Autumn

Now in late autumn
    Look, on my old
     Rubbish-heap . . .
Blue morning-glory

Taigi

pumpkin

After its lid
Is cut, the slick
Seeds and stuck
Wet strings
Scooped out,
Walls scraped
Dry and white,
Face carved, candle
Fixed and lit,

Light creeps
Into the thick
Rind: giving
That dead orange
Vegetable skull
Warm skin, making
A live head
To hold its
Sharp gold grin.

Valerie Worth

acorn

An acorn
Fits perfectly
Into its shingled
Cup, with a stick
Attached
At the top,

Its polished
Nut curves
In the shape
Of a drop, drawn
Down to a thorn
At the tip,

And its heart
Holds folded
Thick white fat
From which
A marvelous
Tree grows up:

I think no better
Invention or
Mechanical trick
Could ever
Be bought
In a shop.

Valerie Worth

Oh! I Ate Them All

Oh! I ate them all
And oh! What a
Stomach-ache . . .
Green stolen apples

Shiki

Apple

At the center, a dark star
wrapped in white.
When you bite, listen
for the crunch of boots on snow,
snow that has ripened. Over it
stretches the red, starry sky.

Nan Fry

Ladybug, Be Good

Summer's over. Work is through.
Lady, get to bed.
Where your tasty meadow grew,
now a stubble rubs instead.

Dream of lice and aphides,
brood on summer scale.
Hide your wings from crystal freeze,
polka dots from bouncing hail.

Shrink from bleak and blizzard whiffs.
Barely breathe: it's best.
Ladybug, no buts and ifs.
Close your shutters, come to rest.

Norma Farber

Harvest

When the corn stands yellow in September,
A red flower ripens and shines among the stalks
And a red silk creeps among the broad ears
And tall tassels lift over all else
    and keep a singing
    to the prairies
    and the wind.

They are the grand lone ones
For they are never saved
    along with the corn:

They are cut down
and piled high
and burned.

Their fire
lights the west in November.

Carl Sandburg

Autumn Leaves

One of the nicest beds I know
isn't a bed of soft white snow,
isn't a bed of cool green grass
after the noisy mowers pass,
isn't a bed of yellow hay
making me itch for half a day—
but autumn leaves in a pile *that* high,
deep, and smelling like fall, and dry.
That's the bed where I like to lie
and watch the flutters of fall go by.

Aileen Fisher

The Leaves Fall Down

One by one the leaves fall down
From the sky come falling one by one
And leaf by leaf the summer is done
One by one by one by one.

Margaret Wise Brown

Leaves

The winds that blow—
        ask them, which leaf of the tree
                will be next to go!

Soseki

The Harvest Moon

The flame-red moon, the harvest moon,
Rolls along the hills, gently bouncing,
A vast balloon,
Till it takes off, and sinks upward
To lie in the bottom of the sky, like a golden doubloon.

The harvest moon has come,
Booming softly through heaven, like a bassoon.
And earth replies all night, like a deep drum.

So people can't sleep,
So they go out where elms and oak trees keep
A kneeling vigil, in a religious hush.
The harvest moon has come!

And all the moonlit cows and all the sheep
Stare up at her, petrified, while the moon,
Filling heaven, as if red hot, comes sailing
Closer and closer like the end of the world

Till the gold fields of stiff wheat
Cry "We are ripe, reap us!" and the rivers
Sweat from the melting hills.

Ted Hughes

Last Green

When plants wither and lose their color,
the growing cycle ends. Some plants will
return the following season. Others drop seeds
that take root and become new plants.
Still others die and become food for the garden.
These poems pay tribute to the green things
that have departed and the new green to come.

Yase: September

Old Mrs. Kawabata
cuts down the tall spike weeds—
        more in two hours
than I can get done in a day.

out of a mountain
of grass and thistle
she saved five dusty stalks
        of ragged wild blue flower
and put them in my kitchen
        in a jar.

Gary Snyder

The Mist and All

I like the fall.
The mist and all.
I like the night owl's
Lonely call—
And wailing sound
Of wind around.

I like the gray
November day,
And bare, dead boughs
That coldly sway
Against my pane.
I like the rain.

I like to sit
And laugh at it—
And tend
My cozy fire a bit.
I like the fall—
The mist and all.—

       Dixie Willson

First White Snow of Fall

First white snow of Fall
   Just enough to bend
   The leaves
Of faded daffodils

      Basho

Maple Sweet

When you see the vapor pillar lick the forest and the sky,
You may know the days of sugar making then are drawing nigh;
Frosty night and sunny day, make the maple pulses play,
Till the overflow of sweetness just begins to drip away.

Chorus
Oh! Bubble, bubble, bubble, bubble goes the pan,
Furnish sweeter music for the season if you can,
See the golden billows, watch their ebb and flow
Sweetest joys indeed, we sugar makers know.

When you see the farmer trudging with the dripping buckets home,
You may know the days of sugar making then have fully come;
As the fragrant odors pour through the open kitchen door,
How the eager children rally, ever loudly calling, "More!"

Do you say you don't believe it? Take a saucer and a spoon
Though you're sourer than a lemon, you'll be sweeter very soon.
Why, the greenest leaves you see, on the spreading maple tree,
Though they sip and sip all summer, will the autumn beauties be.

And for home or love, or any kind of sickness, 'tis the thing,
Take in plentiful doses and repeat it every spring;
Until everyone you meet, if at home or on the street,
Will be half a mind to bite you, for you look so very sweet.

Carl Carmer

The Tree on the Corner

I've seen
the tree on the corner
in spring bud
and summer green.
Yesterday
it was yellow gold.

Then a cold
wind began to blow.
Now I know—
you really do not see
a tree
until you see
its bones.

Lilian Moore

Buds

When all the other leaves are gone
The brown oak leaves still linger on,
Their branches obstinately lifted
To frozen wind and snow deep-drifted.

But when the winter is well passed
The brown oak leaves drop down at last,
To let the little buds appear
No larger than a mouse's ear.

Elizabeth Coatsworth

FOREVER GREEN

The poems about the perils
to our environment make us think about
what we are at risk of losing. The poets and
their poems say, *Let's help protect our
beautiful and generous green Earth!*

Earth

"A planet doesn't explode of itself," said drily
The Martian astronomer, gazing off into the air—
"That they were able to do it is proof that highly
Intelligent beings must have been living there."

John Hall Wheelock

To Nature Seekers

Where the slanting forest eves
Shingled light with greenest leaves
Sweep the scented meadow sedge
Let us snoop along the edge,
Let us pry in hidden nooks
Laden with our nature books,
Scaring birds with happy cries,
Chloroforming butterflies,
Rooting up each woodland plant,
Pinning beetle, fly and ant
So we may identify
What we've ruined by and by.

Robert W. Chambers

Hurt No Living Thing

Hurt no living thing:
  Ladybird, nor butterfly,
Nor moth with dusty wing,
  Nor cricket chirping cheerily,
Nor grasshopper so light of leap,
  Nor dancing gnat, nor beetle fat,
Nor harmless worms that creep.

Christina Rossetti

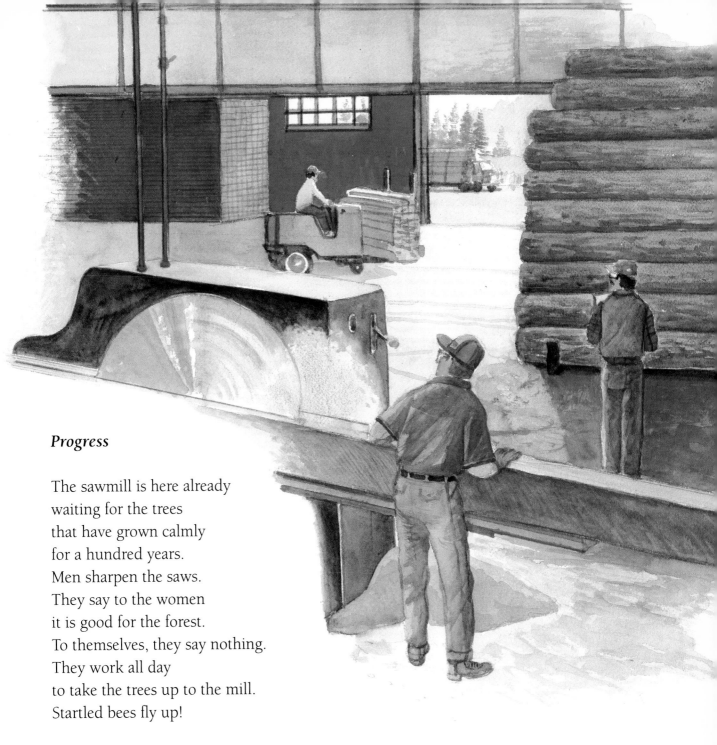

Progress

The sawmill is here already
waiting for the trees
that have grown calmly
for a hundred years.
Men sharpen the saws.
They say to the women
it is good for the forest.
To themselves, they say nothing.
They work all day
to take the trees up to the mill.
Startled bees fly up!

In the houses, women bake bread
to keep from smelling
the heartwood thrown open against the blade.

Connie Martin

And They Lived Happily Ever After for a While

It was down by the Dirty River
  As the Smog was beginning to thin
Because we had been so busy
  Breathing the worst of it in,

That the worst remained inside us
  And whatever we breathed back
Was only—sort of—grayish,
  Or at least not entirely black.

It was down by the Dirty River
  That flows to the Sticky Sea
I gave my heart to Bonnie,
  And she gave hers to me.

I coughed: "I love you, Bonnie.
  And do you love me true?"
The tears of joy flowed from my eyes
  When she sneezed back: "Yes—Achoo!"

66

It was high in the Garbage Mountains,
  In Saint Snivens by the Scent,
I married my darling Bonnie
  And we built our Oxygen Tent.

And here till the tanks are empty
  We sit and watch TV
And dream of the Dirty River
  On its way to the Sticky Sea.

Here till the needles quiver
  Shut on the zero mark
We sit hand in hand while the TV screen
  Shines like a moon in the dark.

I cough: "I love you, Bonnie.
  And do you love me true?"
And tears of joy flow from our eyes
  When she sneezes: "Yes—Achoo!"

John Ciardi

The Flower-Fed Buffaloes

The flower-fed buffaloes of the spring
In the days of long ago,
Ranged where the locomotives sing
And the prairie flowers lie low:—
The tossing, blooming, perfumed grass
Is swept away by wheat,
Wheels and wheels and wheels spin by
In the spring that still is sweet.
But the flower-fed buffaloes of the spring
Left us, long ago.
They gore no more, they bellow no more,
They trundle around the hills no more:—
With the Blackfeet lying low.
With the Pawnees lying low.

Vachel Lindsay

A Prayer for a Carpenter

About most subjects
I am quite elastic,
But I cannot stand
A world of plastic.

Plastic flowers, plastic tables,
Plastic window, plastic door,
Plastic, plastic,
I abhor.

When I die,
And if I'm good,
I pray that heaven
Be built of wood.

Louis Phillips

The Great Auk's Ghost

The Great Auk's ghost rose on one leg,
Sighed thrice and three times winkt,
And turned and poached a phantom egg
And muttered, "I'm extinct."

Ralph Hodgson

Choose a Color

If I were brown I'd be cattail
or turtle deep burrowed
in mud.

If I were orange
I'd be a newt's belly,

If yellow a willow
in Fall.

If pink I'd be a flamingo
or salmon
leaping upstream.

If I were blue
I'd be glacier,

If purple a larkspur
in Spring.

If I were silver
I'm sure I'd be river
    moonshattered
in liquid surprise.

If I were green
I'd be rainforest,

tree canopied.

If green I would help
the world

breathe.

Jacqueline Sweeney

This Pretty Planet (A Round)

This pretty planet
spinning through space,
You're garden,
you're harbor,
you're holy place.

Golden sun going down,
Gentle blue giant,
Spin us around.

All through the night,
Safe til the morning light.

John Forster and Tom Chapin

Valentine for Earth

Oh, it will be fine
To rocket through space
And see the reverse
Of the moon's dark face,

To travel to Saturn
Or Venus or Mars,
Or maybe discover
Some uncharted stars.

But do they have anything
Better than we?
Do you think, for instance,
They have a blue sea

For sailing and swimming?
Do the planets have hills
With raspberry thickets
Where a song sparrow fills

The summer with music?
And do they have snow
To silver the roads
Where the school buses go?

Oh, I'm all for rockets
And worlds cold or hot,
But I'm wild in love
With the planet we've got!

Frances Frost

Index

Authors

A

Anonymous, 2
Austin, Mary, 28
Aztec Indians, 34

B

Basho, 59
Blount, Roy, Jr., 44
Brown, Margaret Wise, 4, 56

C

Carmer, Carl, 61
Chambers, Robert W., 64
Chapin, Tom, and John Forster, 72
Ciardi, John, 46, 66 – 67
Coatsworth, Elizabeth, 62
Coffin, Robert P. Tristram, 26

D

Davies, Mary Carolyn, 18
Dreskin, Leila, 18
Dreskin, Tanya, 7

F

Farber, Norma, 54
Farjeon, Eleanor, 39
Fisher, Aileen, 38, 56
Forster, John, and Tom Chapin, 72
Fraser, Kathleen, 29
Frost, Frances, 73
Fry, Nan, 53

H

Hans, Marcie, 11
Henderson, Harold (translated by), 19
Hoberman, Mary Ann, 5
Hodgson, Ralph, 69
Hughes, Ted, 57

J

Janosco, Beatrice, 41
Joans, Ted, 43

K

Kennedy, X.J., 10, 16
Kumin, Maxine W., 33

L

Lewis, Claudia, 24
Lindsay, Vachel, 68
Livingston, Myra Cohn, 6

M

Martin, Connie, 65
McCord, David, 3, 12, 20 – 21, 37, 48 – 49
Merriam, Eve, 23, 30, 40
Millay, Edna St. Vincent, 25
Moffitt, John, 9
Moore, Lilian, 36, 62
Morrison, Lillian, 8

N
Navajo Indians, 35

O
Onitsura, 13

P
Papago, 34
Peck, Robert Newton, 19, 31
Phillips, Louis, 30, 50, 69
Popa, Vasko, 45
Prelutsky, Jack, 44

R
Reed, Edward Bliss, 22
Roberts, Elizabeth Madox, 17
Roethke, Theodore, 42
Rossetti, Christina, 64
Ryoto, 17

S
Sandburg, Carl, 45, 55
Sanpū, 13
Scheele, Roy, 37
Shiki, 53

S
Sia, 15
Silverstein, Shel, 14
Snyder, Gary, 58
Soseki, 56
Spilka, Arnold, 46
Sweeney, Jacqueline, 70 — 71

T
Taggard, Genevieve, 47
Taigi, 51

W
Wallace, Robert, 38
Wheelock, John Hall, 63
Willson, Dixie, 59
Withers, Carl, 43
Worth, Valerie, 32, 50, 52, 53

Z
Zolotow, Charlotte, 29, 39
Zuni Corn Ceremony, 35

TITLES

A

Accidentally, 33
acorn, 53
And They Lived Happily Ever
    After for a While, 66 – 67
Apple, 53
Autumn Leaves, 56
Azalea, 29

B

Be Different to Trees, 18
Blow-up, 16
Blue Magic, 39
Buds, 62

C

Choose a Color, 70 – 71
Comb of Trees, The, 24
Corn Grows Up, The, 35
Counting-out Rhyme, 25

D

dandelion, 32
Deep Green Forest, The, 7
Directions, 13

E

Earth, 63
Earth Song, 3
Evergreen, 23

F

First One Out of Bed, 10
First White Snow of Fall, 59
Five Chants, 20 – 21
Flower-Fed Buffaloes, The, 68
Flowers at Night, 38
Fueled, 11

G

Garden Hose, The, 41
Gopher in the Garden, A, 44

Grass

Grass, 29
Grass on the Mountain, The, 28
Great Auk's Ghost, The, 69
Green Song, 8
Green Stems, 4
Green With Envy, 30

H

Harvest, 55
Harvest Moon, The, 57
Hurt No Living Thing, 64

I

I Don't Know Why, 6
I'm Glad . . . , 2
Is It Raining Up There, 34

K

Kudzu, 40

L

Ladybug, Be Good, 54
lawnmower, 50
Leaves, 56
Leaves Fall Down, The, 56

M

Man in the Onion Bed, The, 46
Maple Sweet, 61
Millions of Strawberries, 47
Mist and All, The, 59
Moss, The, 18
Mr. Bidery's Spidery Garden, 48 – 49
Mushrooms, 31
Mushrooms Are Umbrellas, 46

N

Nicely, Nicely, 35
Nocturn Cabbage, 45
Now in Late Autumn, 51

O

Oak Leaf Plate, 5
Oh! I Ate Them All, 53
On the Problem of Growing a Head
    of Lettuce in a Very Small Garden, 30

P

Poison Ivy, 50
Poplars, 22
Poppies, 37
Potato, 45
Prayer for a Carpenter, A, 69
Progress, 65
pumpkin, 52

S

Silver Lining, 13
Snowman, 14
Song Against Broccoli, 44
Song of a Dream, The, 34
Spring Talk, 12
Strange Houses, 43
Strange Tree, 17
Sumac Whistle, 19

T

Tempter, The, 19
This Pretty Planet (A Round), 72
Tiger Lily, 37
To Look at Any Thing, 9
To Nature Seekers, 64
Tree on the Corner, The, 62
Tree-Sleeping, 26
Tulip, 38
Two Ancient Pine-Trees, 17

V

Valentine for Earth, 73
Violets, 39

W

Waking, The, 42
Watermelon, 43
weeds, 32
White Floating Clouds, 15

Y

Yase: September, 58
Yellow Weed, 36

FIRST LINES

A

About most subjects, 69
After its lid, 52
An acorn, 53
"A planet doesn't explode of itself," said drily, 63
April's here, to cut for me, 19
At the center, a dark star, 53
Away beyond the Jarboe house, 17

C

Cabbages catch at the moon, 45

E

Every time I climb a tree, 20—21
Eyes, side to side, 13

F

First white snow of Fall, 59
Fueled, 11

G

Grass!, 29

H

Hemlock and pine, 23
How did you get here, 36
Hurt no living thing, 64

I

"I," 30
I can never get my fill, 8
I don't know why, 6
I feel as though, 29
If I were brown I'd be cattail, 70—71
I like the fall, 59
I met a man in an onion bed, 46
I'm glad the sky is painted blue, 2
In the gray evening, 41
In the rough places, 32
In the woods the bluebells seem, 39
I strolled across, 42
It digs the air with green blades, 38
It is raining up there, 34
Its got a good shape/the outside color is green/
        its one of them foods from Africa, 43

It was down by the Dirty River, 66—67
I've seen, 62

J

Jack-in-the-pulpit: Where are you, Jack?, 12

L

Let me dry you, says the desert, 3
Little lowly people of the earth, 31
Little things that crawl and creep, 4

M

Marcia and I went over the curve, 47
May rains pour, 13
Mushrooms are umbrellas, 46
Mysterious murky, 45

N

Nicely, nicely, nicely, away in the east, 35
Now in late autumn, 51
Now, my friends, please hear, 34

O

Oak leaf plate, 5
Oh! I ate them all, 53
Oh, it will be fine, 73
Oh, long long, 28
Old Mrs. Kawabata, 58
Once—I didn't mean to, 33
Once there was a tree, 18
One by one the leaves fall down, 56
One of the nicest beds I know, 56
Our cherry tree, 16
Out of, 32

P

Personally, 50
Plum blossoms swaying, 19
Poor old Mr. Bidery, 48—49

R

Rapid, 30
Riding to Rock Creek, 24

S

Silver bark of beech, and sallow, 25
Some flowers close their petals, 38
Someone is coming, 39
Summer's over. Work is through, 54

T

The corn grows up, 35
The deep green forest is dark and quiet, 7
The flame-red moon, the harvest moon, 57
The flower-fed buffaloes of the spring, 68
The Great Auk's ghost rose on one leg, 69
The lawnmower, 50
The light in them stands as clear as water, 37
The local groceries are all out of broccoli, 44
The poplar is a lonely tree, 22
There's a gopher in the garden, and he's eating all
    the onions, 44
There was a little green house, 43
The sawmill is here already, 65
The talking oak, 18

The tiger lily is a panther, 37
The winds that blow——, 56
This pretty planet, 72
To look at any thing, 9
'Twas the first day of the springtime, 14
Two ancient pine-trees, 17

U

Up through the ground, 10

W

When all the other leaves are gone, 62
When I was small and trees were high, 26
When kudzu seed the sower sows, 40
When the corn stands yellow in September, 55
When you see the vapor pillar lick the forest
    and the sky, 61
Where the slanting forest eves, 64
White floating clouds, 15

Acknowledgments

Grateful acknowledgment is made to the following authors, agents, and publishers for the use of copyrighted material. Every effort has been made to obtain permission to use previously published material. Any errors or omissions are unintentional.

American Folklore Society for "The Corn Grows Up." Reproduced by permission of the American Folklore Society from *Journal of American Folklore*, Volume VII, 1984. Not for further reproduction.

Anvil Press Poetry. "Potato" is from *Vasko Popa: Complete Poems*, translated by Anne Pennington, revised and expanded by Francis R. Jones, and published by Anvil Press Poetry in 1993.

Bantam Doubleday Dell Publishing Group, Inc. "Leaves," "Silver Lining," "Directions," and "The Tempter." From *An Introduction to Haiku*, by Harold G. Henderson. Copyright ©1958 by Harold G. Henderson. Used by permission of Doubleday, a division of Bantam Doubleday Dell Publishing Group, Inc. "The Waking," copyright ©1953 by Theodore Roethke. From *The Collected Poems of Theodore Roethke*, by Theodore Roethke. Used by permission of Doubleday, a division of Bantam Doubleday Dell Publishing Group, Inc.

Elizabeth Barnett. "Counting-out Rhyme," by Edna St. Vincent Millay. From *Collected Poems*, Harper & Row. Copyright ©1928, 1955 by Edna St. Vincent Millay and Norma Millay Ellis. Reprinted by permission of Elizabeth Barnett, literary executor.

Dana W. Briggs for "The Mist and All," by Dixie Willson. From *Child Life* magazine. Copyright © 1924, 1952 by Rand McNally and Company.

Curtis Brown, Ltd. for "Accidentally," from *No One Writes a Letter to the Snail*. Reprinted by permission of Curtis Brown, Ltd. Copyright © 1962 by Maxine W. Kumin.

Bryn Mawr College. "The Great Auk's Ghost," by Ralph Hodgson, from *The Moon Is Shining Bright as Day*, © Lippincott,1953. By permission of Bryn Mawr College, Pennsylvania.

Carnegie Mellon University for "Tulip." Reprinted from *Swimmer in the Rain*, by Robert Wallace. By permission of Carnegie Mellon University Press ©1979.

Tom Chapin and John Forster for "This Pretty Planet" © 1988, Limousine Music Co. Last Music Co. (ASCAP).

Judith H. Ciardi. "The Man in the Onion Bed," from *I Met a Man* ©1961 Houghton Mifflin. Permission granted by Judith H. Ciardi. "And They Lived Happily Ever After for a While," from

Fast & Slow © 1975 Houghton Mifflin. Permission granted by Judith H. Ciardi.

Leila Dreskin for "The Moss," by Leila Dreskin. Used by permission of the author.
Tanya Dreskin for "The Deep Green Forest," by Tanya Dreskin. Used by permission of the author.

Farrar, Straus & Giroux, Inc. "The Song of a Dream," from *In the Trail of the Wind*, by John Bierhorst. Copyright © 1971 by John Bierhorst. Reprinted by permission of Farrar, Straus & Giroux, Inc. "lawnmower," "acorn," "pumpkin," and "weeds," from *More Small Poems*, by Valerie Worth. Copyright ©1976 by Valerie Worth. Reprinted by permission of Farrar, Straus & Giroux, Inc. "dandelion," from *Small Poems Again*, by Valerie Worth. Copyright ©1975 by Valerie Worth. Reprinted by permission of Farrar, Straus & Giroux, Inc.

Aileen Fisher for "Flowers at Night" and "Autumn Leaves," from *In the Woods, In the Meadow, In the Sky*, Scribners, N.Y. 1965.

Harcourt Brace Jovanovich, Inc. "Fueled," from *Serve Me a Slice of Moon*, copyright ©1965 by Marcie Hans, reprinted by permission of Harcourt Brace Jovanovich, Inc. "Harvest," from *Honey and Salt*, copyright © 1963 by Carl Sandburg and renewed 1991 by Margaret Sandburg, Janet Sandburg, and Helga Sandburg Crile, reprinted by permission of Harcourt Brace Jovanovich, Inc. "Nocturn Cabbage," from *Good Morning, America*, copyright © 1928 and renewed 1956 by Carl Sandburg, reprinted by permission of Harcourt Brace Jovanovich, Inc.

HarperCollins Publishers. Selection: "Green Stems" and "The Leaves Fall Down" text from *Nibble, Nibble*, by Margaret Wise Brown. Text copyright ©1959 by William R. Scott, Inc. Renewed 1987 by Roberta Brown Rauch. Selection reprinted by permission of HarperCollins Publishers. Selection: "Snowman" text from *Where the Sidewalk Ends*, by Shel Silverstein. Copyright © 1974 by Evil Eye Music, Inc. Selection reprinted by permission of HarperCollins Publishers. "Azalea" and "Violets" from *River Winding* © 1970 by Charlotte Zolotow. Reproduced by permission of HarperCollins Publishers. "The Comb of Trees," by Claudia Lewis. Copyright © 1991 by Claudia Lewis. From *Up in the Mountains: And Other Poems of Long Ago*. Reprinted by permission of HarperCollins Publishers.

Henry Holt and Company, Inc. for "Strange Houses." From *I Saw a Rocket Walk a Mile* by Carl Withers. Copyright ©1965 by Carl Withers. Reprinted by permission of Henry Holt and Company, Inc.

Houghton Mifflin Company. "The Grass on the Mountain," from *The American Rhythm* by Mary Austin. Copyright © renewed 1958 by Kenneth M. Chapman and Mary C.